The HIVE

Is a Book
We Read
For its Honey

poems by
GERRY GRUBBS

DOS MADRES
2013

"We are the bees of the invisible. We wildly collect the honey of the visible, to store it in the great golden hive of the invisible."

Rainer Maria Rilke
–translated by Stephen Mitchell

DOS MADRES PRESS INC.
P.O.Box 294, Loveland, Ohio 45140
www.dosmadres.com   editor@dosmadres.com

Dos Madres is dedicated to the belief that the small press is essential to the vitality of contemporary literature as a carrier of the new voice, as well as the older, sometimes forgotten voices of the past. And in an ever more virtual world, to the creation of fine books pleasing to the eye and hand.

Dos Madres is named in honor of Vera Murphy and Libbie Hughes, the "Dos Madres" whose contributions have made this press possible.

Dos Madres Press, Inc. is an Ohio Not For Profit Corporation and a 501 (c) (3) qualified public charity. Contributions are tax deductible.

Executive Editor: Robert J. Murphy

Illustration & Book Design: Elizabeth H. Murphy
www.illusionstudios.net

Typset in Adobe Garamond Pro &Bookman Old Style
ISBN 978-1-939929-04-4
Library of Congress Control Number: 2013944059

First Edition

Copyright 2013 Dos Madres Press inc.
All rights to reproduction of the text, quotation, and translation reside with the author.

For Mary

Table of Contents

Warning..............1

I Hive

Sometime in the Evening..............5
Studies in the Advanced Architecture of Desire..............6
Disturb the Bees..............7
Location..............8
Apoidea..............9
Whisper..............10
The Distance..............11
The Heart..............12
That Boy..............13
Sing..............14
We Want so Much..............15
Give..............16

II The Universe is a Bee..............17

III Flowers

Fragrance and Flowering..............33
Each Flower..............34
In What Direction..............35
Rose..............36
There Was A Flower..............37
Blue Flower Haiku..............38
Your Life..............39
Day..............40
Night..............41

IV Following the Fragrance of the Night

Seeking..............45
These Three Things..............46
Celebration..............47
Honey..............48
Night..............49
Full Moon..............50
How to Lose Something..............51
Memory..............52
Apple Blossom Dream..............53
In the Orchard..............54
Apple Blossoms..............55

Acknowledgements and Dedications..............57

Warning

Approach the hive with caution
As if approaching sacred ground
With the attendant smoke
And humility
In this way the bees grow drowsy
Allowing safe access to the honey
Each moment
Can be approached in this manner
Its honey extracted for your nourishment
For your gain

I

HIVE

Sometimes in the Evening

Sometimes in the evening
When the sun lies down
On the horizon as if to take
It all into itself
Trying to turn each corner
Of the world into light
I think it has turned
Into roses and fire
And I think of the bees
Who would finish the work
Taking that fire
Back to the hive
I think of the hive burning
Of that red honey
Dripping like the petals
It was stolen from
I think of that little thief
Who desires to disappear
Into the night
But cannot
For its wings
Are full of light

Studies in the Advanced Architecture of Desire

The orange blossom

The bee
Loud
In the face of beauty
All afternoon

The back of your lovers
Left shoulder
In the light
Of the first full moon
Of summer

Years from now
Should these few words survive
And you are reading them
That flame that rises
And flickers
And never dies

Disturb the Bees

A few words
Can disturb the bees
A few thoughts
Can disturb the flowers
It is enough
To watch them
Serenely touching
Giving what effort is required
Mindful of each dip and buzz
Look how they practice
Meditating on each other
Cultivating the wisdom of honey
Avoiding unnecessary discussions
Leaving only when
The work is done

Location

A man alone in the orchard
Walks under the branches
Heavy with fruit
Or with potential fruit

The thin grass beneath his feet
Lets him know what the earth
Looks like in all kinds of weather

Time unfolds from its pocket
Like a map on which the stars
Try to locate him the way bees

Locate the blossoms
From which they spin
Their rich honey

Apoidea

Upon what does the bee depend
With its tongue like water
And its pocket knife mouth

Its multichambered heart
In its abdomen sends colorless
Blood over every organ in its fat body

Flying splinter molting thumb
How long have you been hunting
The source of sweetness
In this flowering world

Whisper

I want to whisper
In your ear
The exact word
That will make
Everything sweet
The way the bee
Whispers its love
In the ear
Of the flower

The Distance

The distance
Between the
flower
And the hive
Is written
In honey

It is the story
Of the heart
Continually filling
Never being full

The Heart

How many times
Can you turn away
Before the heart
Gets hard all the way
Through like a stone

What does the world become then
Do the oceans and lakes
Themselves become hardened

Do the flowers become indifferent

And does the heart retain
The memory of something real
The way a bee retains
Its perfect form
Hardened inside centuries of amber

That Boy

That boy
With his pockets
Full of bees
Thought he
Could make
His own
Honey that way

He does not know
His suffering
Will never be
Greater than
It is right now
That no failure
Will be
So complete
As his realization
That he has
No flowers

Sing

I wanted to sing
The way Neruda sang
About the sea
And the open spaces

But I did not have
A blue watch
Or a star
The color of charcoal
To mark the small white pages
Inside my tiny heart

So I thought I could sing
The way the leaves do
Singing a small green song
All summer long
Reaching that red crescendo
Of autumn but I found
I could not let go
The way leaves
Surrender all

So I looked for something smaller
That could fit inside
The small flower
Of my heart
And found there
A bee full of light
Ready to make me sing
Of its golden honey

We Want so Much

The hive is a book
Read for its honey

We want so much

We cultivate them
In white boxes out back

Or in the tops of tall trees
The way the honey men do
Those whose wealth
Is measured in bees

And for those able
To follow a bee in the dark
There is wild honey waiting
To satisfy them

Give

Give me the clamoring
Give me the end of day
Give me the stars
Too tired to shine
Give me the abandoned light
Give me the last bee
Returning to the hive
Give me the dark honey
Night gives those who stay
Give me the branch
With her flowering children
Give me the flavor
That is flavoring the night
Give me the tinsel
Give me the shine

II

The Universe is a Bee

The universe is a bee
A small golden thing
Hovering in the midst
Of a great darkness
As if straining
To let there be light
Flickering wings
Throwing off sparks

The universe is a bee
And each eye of the bee is a bee
And each wing is a bee
It is a bee of bees
Each bee the same
With bees for eyes and
Bees for wings and so on
Each spark that flies
From its bee wings
Is a bee of light
A river of light
Is a river of bees

There are bees hidden in the bees
And bees hidden in the honey
Honey hidden in the bees
Hiding in the honey
And hiding in the bees

The bee is a mind serene

That hum you hear now….

Is the bee
At the center
Of everything

In the beginning
Night opened a window
And let out its own light
And called it a bee

Nothing was made
That was made
Without the bee

And the bee said
Let there be hives
And there were hives
And the bee saw
That they were good

There are bees hidden
In the mountains
Among the cliffs
Hives hidden in the trees
And hives hidden
In the ground
And in the rocky places
And in the walls
There is honey hidden
In the mountains and
Among the caves
Hidden in the ground
And in many places

The bee is a mind
That moves in beauty

The universe is a bee
That hovers above
That dark flower
Taking what it is given
Turning it into light

Oh bee of the universe
Give us the light
Necessary to find
Your dark honey

III

Flowers

Fragrance and Flowering

Where do we go from here if not to the tulips
And chrysanthemums what else is there
But the earth and rain and the longing for light
If everything came to be because it was spoken
These must be the softest words calling us
To live where all is fragrance and flowering

Each Flower

Each flower
Must be approached
Individually

You cannot reach
To touch the waxy
Surface until it is ready

And if she wants you
To touch her hand
She will tell you
Where her thorns
Are hidden
She will let you
Catch the dew drop
Rolling down
The petal of her cheek

In What Direction

In what direction
Does the rose point
When it is completely open

Rose

This is my version
Of paradise
And you are in it
And a woman
Reading
So slowly
That each word
Lasts forever

And when she says Rose
You are caught
On the thorn
Of the first letter
For what seems
Like a lifetime

Until you see
Her perfect lips
Forming that pure
Round
Infinity of the O
And all the pain
Is forgotten
And you no longer
Remember
What comes next

There was a Flower

There was a flower
In this field
Yesterday

I wish I had
Seen who collected it

She must have taken it
For its beauty and size

Or maybe for
The fragrance
So strong
It still lingers
For a little while

I wonder
What comes next

What the empty space
Waits for

I think I'll wait
And see

Blue Flower Haiku

Seventeen blue flowers
Floating
Into this world
And back
Out again

Your Life

What is a flower
Other than
The unending night
Blooming now
In your chest
With the texture
Of a dove
And that yellow
Stamen shinning
Like all the stars
Guiding you
Toward the fragrance
Of your life

Day

The day is like a woman
With so many lovers
She no longer remembers their names
But smiles as she takes in
The fragrance from all the flowers
They have gathered just for her

Night

Night is a fragrance
That gives rise to itself
Causing us to search
For something
That is not there
A night blooming flower
That never blooms
Never fades
Never wilts
Never dies

IV

Following the Fragrance of the Night

The vast night
Now nothing left
But the fragrance
Jorge Luis Borges

Searching

Seeking
What has always been sought
The small stream
Moves toward the sea

These Three Things

These three things
Always undo me
The starry night
The scent of the sea
And the unexpected
Logic of the rose

Celebration

In the great galaxies
All the sparkle belongs

From the tightest center

To the last strand of pearls flung

Here it is not you or I

All is one
Bright moment
In the midst
Of nights
Only celebration

Honey

Inside me
It feels
As if
The bees
Have begun
Turning
What's been
Brought back
Into honey
Filling
The dark comb
Of my soul
With thick light

Night

Night has the darkest petals
For the one who calls his own name
Who is unable to believe
And so remains lost looking
For the one who called
Wondering how a flower that dark
Could know his name

Full Moon

My heart
Remembers
All those nights

How to Lose Something

Let someone else
Tell you how
It is supposed to be done

Follow those vague instructions
Until you run out of words

Finding yourself alone
In the woods
You will believe
You came this way
For some good reason

And so you begin
The gathering of things
You find along the way

All the time
Believing you had something
But can't remember what

Memory

What is shadow
Other than light
Remembering the place
From which it was removed

Apple Blossom Dream

I dreamed
I was in the orchard
In spring
The bees busy
Passing secrets
Back and forth
Between the apple
Blossoms
When I fell asleep
Within my dream
And when I awoke
From my second sleep
There was only
The fragrance
Of those blossoms
Gathered like worshipers
Of the moon
And the moon
Was giving
All its light to them

In the Orchard

If you find yourself in the orchard
Before dawn listening to what
The blossoms spread in anticipation
Of some other arrival ask yourself
If there is anything more important
Then this moment in the dark
Alone among the trees whose fragrance
Is calling for the dawn to come

Apple blossoms

There are bees among the apple blossoms

Those pink and white dresses the trees create

For their thin branches every spring

The bees come because of the fragrance that invites

They are attracted to the sudden appearance

Of this nourishing beauty in the receding gray of winter

But there is more happening here unseen

Like those who study sacred text soon discover

The fruit we desire soon begins to grow

The trees in our orchards fill with it

An abundance we share with others

Not entirely of our own making

What Question
Does the bee
Continually pose
To the flower
Whose answer
Is always sweetness

Acknowledgements and Dedications

Many of these poems first appeared in the following publications, whose editors I thank:

Laughing Dog, *Diamond Dust*, *Mudfish*, *Cincinnati Express*, *Peace and Justice 2012* and *Big Muddy*.

"Seeking what has always been sought" was published in the *2nd Annual Basho Haiku Challenge*.

1) This book is dedicated to David Leonard whose enthusiasm for some of the Bee poems inspired this collection.

2) "Rose" is for Carissa Craven.

3) "There was a Flower" is in memory of Brian Heller.

4) "Honey" is for Virginia Burroughs.

5) "The Universe is a Bee" is dedicated to Jeanine Mamary.

ABOUT THE AUTHOR

He has a previous book from Dos Madres Press, *The Girls in Bright Dresses Dancing*, as well as a book from Wordtech, *Palaces of the Night*.

He has poems appearing or previously published in *The Painted Bride Quarterly, Poet Lore, The Cream City Review, Laughing Dog, Mudfish* and other small magazines.

He has developed a unique approach to poetry workshops called Wordshop which he conducts through the year all across the country.

He practices law in Cincinnati.
He can be reached by email at ggrubbs@fuse.net

Books by Dos Madres Press

Mary Margaret Alvarado - *Hey Folly* (2013)
John Anson - *Jose-Maria de Heredia's Les Trophées* (2013)
Jennifer Arin - *Ways We Hold* (2012)
Michael Autrey - *From The Genre Of Silence* (2008)
Paul Bray - *Things Past and Things to Come* (2006), *Terrible Woods* (2008)
Jon Curley - *New Shadows* (2009), *Angles of Incidents* (2012)
Sara Dailey - *Earlier Lives* (2012)
Richard Darabaner - *Plaint* (2012)
Deborah Diemont - *Wanderer* (2009), *Diverting Angels* (2012)
Joseph Donahue - *The Copper Scroll* (2007)
Annie Finch - *Home Birth* (2004)
Norman Finkelstein - *An Assembly* (2004), *Scribe* (2009)
Gerry Grubbs - *Still Life* (2005), *Girls in Bright Dresses Dancing* (2010)
Ruth D. Handel - *Tugboat Warrior* (2013)
Richard Hague - *Burst, Poems Quickly* (2004),
    During The Recent Extinctions (2012)
Pauletta Hansel - *First Person* (2007), *What I Did There* (2011)
Michael Heller - *A Look at the Door with the Hinges Off* (2006),
    Earth and Cave (2006)
Michael Henson - *The Tao of Longing & The Body Geographic* (2010)
R. Nemo Hill - *When Men Bow Down* (2012)
W. Nick Hill - *And We'd Understand Crows Laughing* (2012)
Eric Hoffman - *Life At Braintree* (2008), *The American Eye* (2011),
    By The Hours (2013)
James Hogan - *Rue St. Jacques* (2005)
Keith Holyoak - *My Minotaur* (2010), *Foreigner* (2012)
David M. Katz - *Claims of Home* (2011)
Burt Kimmelman - *There Are Words* (2007), *The Way We Live* (2011)
Pamela L. Laskin - *Plagiarist* (2012)
Richard Luftig - *Off The Map* (2006)
Austin MacRae - *The Organ Builder* (2012)
J. Morris - *The Musician, Approaching Sleep* (2006)
Rick Mullin - *Soutine* (2012), *Coelacanth* (2013)
Robert Murphy - *Not For You Alone* (2004), *Life in the Ordovician* (2007),
    From Behind The Blind (2013)

Pam O'Brien - *The Answer To Each Is The Same* (2012)
Peter O'Leary - *A Mystical Theology of the Limbic Fissure* (2005)
Bea Opengart - *In The Land* (2011)
David A. Petreman - *Candlelight in Quintero - bilingual edition* (2011)
Paul Pines - *Reflections in a Smoking Mirror* (2011), *New Orleans Variations & Paris Ouroboros* (2013)
David Schloss - *Behind the Eyes* (2005)
William Schickel - *What A Woman* (2007)
Lianne Spidel & Anne Loveland - *Pairings* (2012)
Murray Shugars - *Songs My Mother Never Taught Me* (2011), *Snakebit Kudzu* (2013)
Olivia Stiffler - *Otherwise, we are safe* (2013)
Carole Stone - *Hurt, the Shadow- the Josephine Hopper poems* (2013)
Nathan Swartzendruber - *Opaque Projectionist* (2009)
Jean Syed - *Sonnets* (2009)
Madeline Tiger - *The Atheist's Prayer* (2010), *From the Viewing Stand* (2011)
James Tolan - *Red Walls* (2011)
Henry Weinfield - *The Tears of the Muses* (2005), *Without Mythologies* (2008), *A Wandering Aramaean* (2012)
Donald Wellman - *A North Atlantic Wall* (2010), *The Cranberry Island Series* (2012)
Anne Whitehouse - *The Refrain* (2012)
Martin Willetts Jr. - *Secrets No One Must Talk About* (2011)
Tyrone Williams - *Futures, Elections* (2004), *Adventures of Pi* (2011)
Kip Zegers - *The Poet of Schools* (2013)

www.dosmadres.com